Piano Technique

Authors
Barbara Kreader, Fred Kern, Phillip Keveren, Mona Rejino

Editor
Carol Klose

Illustrator
Fred Bell

ISBN 978-0-634-01355-3

Visit Hal Leonard Online at
www.halleonard.com

World headquarters, contact:
Hal Leonard
7777 West Bluemound Road
Milwaukee, WI 53213
Email: info@halleonard.com

In Europe, contact:
Hal Leonard Europe Limited
1 Red Place
London, W1K 6PL
Email: info@halleonardeurope.com

In Australia, contact:
Hal Leonard Australia Pty. Ltd.
4 Lentara Court
Cheltenham, Victoria, 3192 Australia
Email: info@halleonard.com.au

Dear Teacher,

Piano Technique Book 3 presents a *Warm-Up* and an *Etude* for each new technical skill students will encounter in **Piano Lessons Book 3**.

We suggest that you demonstrate each *Warm-Up*. Teaching by demonstration allows students to focus on the purely physical aspects of learning a new skill, such as hand and body position, or arm and finger movement. This helps them understand the connection between the movement they make and the sound they create.

Once students have learned the physical skill presented in each *Warm-Up*, they can use it to play the corresponding *Etude* with expression.

The *Musical Fitness Plan* on each warm-up page teaches new technical concepts and provides a checklist for technical readiness:

- *Legato* and *Staccato*
- **Playing Hands Together**
- **Playing in Extended Position**
- **Playing Chords**
- **Using the Damper Pedal**
- **Changing Positions**
- **Playing Hand over Hand Arpeggios**
- **Playing Black and White Keys Together in the Same Hand**
- **Balance between Melody and Accompaniment**

By the end of **Piano Technique Book 3**, students will be able to play hands together using a variety of finger combinations and articulations, and will have experienced playing in extended position. They will also know six major and minor five-finger patterns and triads, and how to move from one five-finger position to another. Having mastered these skills, students will have the confidence to move on to the technical challenges presented in **Piano Lessons Book 4**.

Best wishes,

Barbara Kreader   Fred Kern

Phillip Keveren   Mona Rejino

Dear Students,

You need an exercise plan to stay physically fit.

Like participating in sports, playing the piano is a physical activity that uses your whole body. **Piano Technique Book 3** will outline the *Musical Fitness Plan* you need to develop new musical skills.

Your *Musical Fitness Plan* includes:

- **Warm-Ups** – drills to develop new musical skills
- **Etudes** – music to practice using the new skills you learned in the *Warm-Ups*

It feels good to play the piano! Your teacher will show you how to play each *Warm-Up*. Follow the *Musical Fitness Plan*, paying careful attention to the way you use your body, arms, and fingers to create music. When you play, notice how the movement you make affects the sound you create. Once you have learned each *Warm-Up*, read and practice the matching *Etude*.

You are now ready to begin.

Have fun!

Barbara Kreader   Fred Kern

Phillip Keveren   Mona Rejino

Piano Technique
Book 3

CONTENTS

*✔

Students can check activities as they complete them.

Musical Fitness Review

Use the following checklist to demonstrate the skills you learned in **Book 2**.

☐ **Sitting at the Piano**

☐ **Hand Position**
Raise your hand and wave to your teacher with your fingers. Notice how your fingers move from the knuckles (bridge). As you press each key, play from the bridge of the hand with each finger.

☐ **Beautiful Tone**

☐ **Attention to Silence**

☐ **Playing Different Dynamic Levels**
pp - p - mp - mf - f - ff

☐ **Playing *Crescendo* and *Decrescendo***
Gradually change the sound from soft to loud or loud to soft by pressing the key to the bottom of the key bed with increasing or decreasing arm weight. Listen to the sound you create.

☐ **Connected Tones – *Legato***
Pass the sound smoothly from finger to finger or hand to hand. Begin each phrase with a downward motion of the arm and end the phrase with an upward motion of the wrist.

☐ **Detached Tones – *Staccato***
Release the key as soon as you play it, letting your wrist bounce lightly. Notice how your finger naturally rebounds and comes to rest on the key.

☐ **Accents**
Drop full arm weight into the key to emphasize a single note.

☐ **Playing Hands Together**
- Parallel motion
- Contrary motion
- Oblique motion
- Different fingers in each hand
- Holding a note in one hand and playing *legato* or *staccato* in the other

☐ **Playing Black and White Keys Together**
When moving from a white key to a black key, move your hand slightly forward for comfort.

Procession
Review Etude

Using all the confidence you gained in **Piano Technique Book 2**, celebrate your new musical skills!
Play each phrase beginning with a downward motion of the arm and ending with an upward motion of the wrist.

With dignity

Accompaniment (Student plays two octaves higher than written.)

With dignity (♩ = 120)

5

Musical Fitness Plan

Use this checklist to review fitness skills and to focus on learning new ones.

- ☐ **Hand Position**

- ☐ **Beautiful Tone**

- ☐ **Attention to Silence**

- ☐ **Playing Different Dynamic Levels**
  - *Mezzo Forte*
  - *Piano*

- ☐ **Playing *Crescendo* and *Decrescendo***

- ☐ **Connected Tones – *Legato***

- ☐ **Detached Tones – *Staccato***

- ☐ **Playing Hands Together**
  - Parallel motion
  - Contrary motion

To the Teacher: *Demonstrate these warm-ups first. This will allow students to focus on the purely physical aspects of learning a new skill. Encourage students to play each warm-up in different octaves.*

Warm-Ups

Rebound *pg. 8*

When you drop a basketball, you release it with a downward motion of your arm. When it rebounds, it causes an upward motion of the wrist.

When playing the *staccato* notes in **Rebound,** let your wrists bounce lightly. Notice how your fingers naturally rebound and come to rest on the keys.

Horn Choir *pg. 9*

Horn players make a legato *sound by playing several notes using one breath. They create a* crescendo/decrescendo *sound by increasing and decreasing the strength of the air flow.*

Imitate the sound of breath moving through a horn by keeping your fingers close to the keys and pressing each one to the bottom of the key bed. Imitate the horn player's increasing and decreasing air flow by varying your arm weight.

Rebound

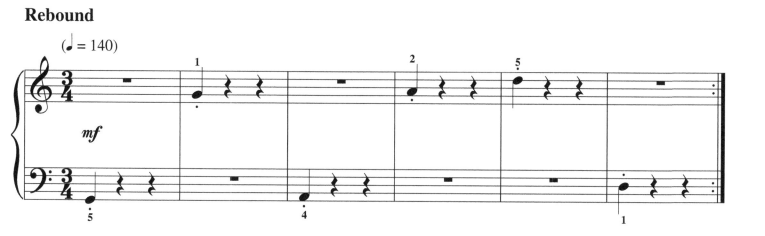

Horn Choir

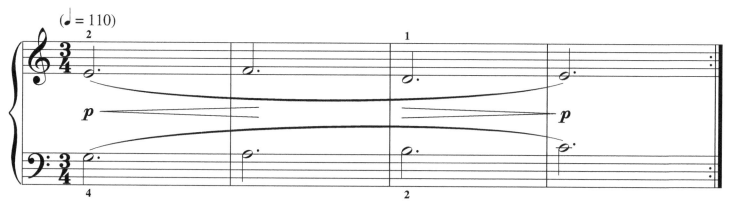

Rebound

Accompaniment (Student plays two octaves higher than written.)

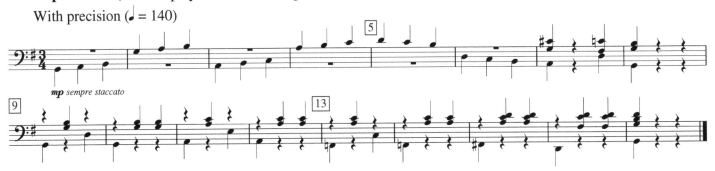

Horn Choir

Andante

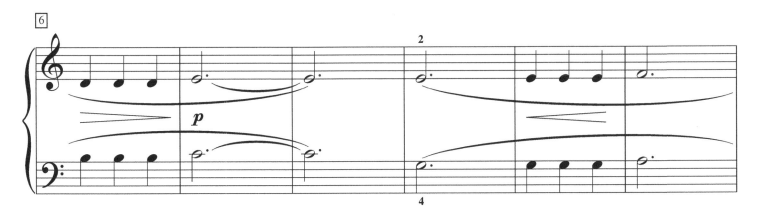

Accompaniment (Student plays one octave higher than written.)

Andante ($\quarternote$ = 110)

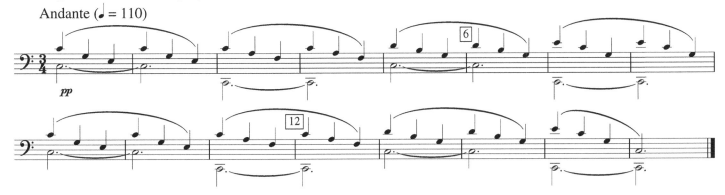

9

Musical Fitness Plan

Use this checklist to review fitness skills and to focus on learning new ones.

- ☐ **Hand Position**

- ☐ **Beautiful Tone**

- ☐ **Attention to Silence**

- ☐ **Playing Different Dynamic Levels**
  - *Mezzo Forte*
  - *Mezzo Piano*
  - *Piano*

- ☐ **Playing *Crescendo* and *Decrescendo***

- ☐ **Connected Tones – *Legato***

- ☐ **Playing Hands Together**

NEW!

Playing in Extended Position
Sometimes it is necessary to extend outside a five-finger position to play a note above or below that position. Let your hand expand slightly as you shift outward with either your thumb or your fifth finger.

Warm-Ups

Rubber Band *pg. 12*

A rubber band can expand and contract. After you extend it, the rubber band returns to its original shape.

Right Hand: Rest your thumb on C, and extend your fifth finger from G up to A, and then back to G.

Left Hand: Rest your fifth finger on C, and extend your thumb from G up to A, and then back to G.

In each hand, let your wrist shift slightly, following the movement of your finger as you play the two upper keys.

E-I-E-I-O *pg. 13*

*The familiar left-hand pattern in **E-I-E-I-O** uses Swing (uneven) eighths:*

long - short long - short   long - short long - short

To play, center the weight of your left hand over finger 2, and rotate your wrist from left to right – from finger 5 to finger 1.

When playing a long *crescendo* or *decrescendo*, change the dynamics gradually.

Rubber Band

E-I-E-I-O

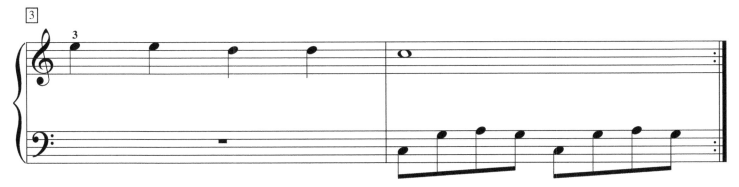

Rubber Band

Slowly

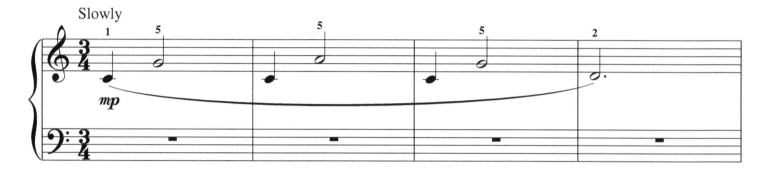

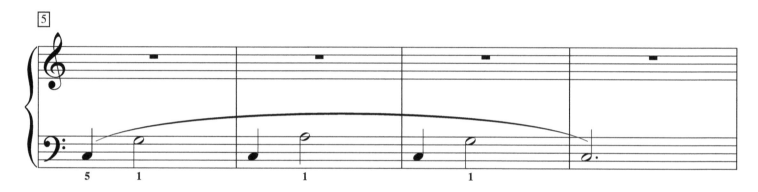

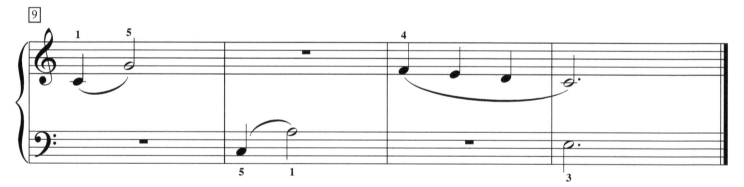

Accompaniment (Student plays two octaves higher than written.)

Slowly (♩ = 100)

p With pedal

E-I-E-I-O

With a swing (♩ = 100)

Use with Lesson Book 3, pgs. 12-13

Musical Fitness Plan

Use this checklist to review fitness skills and to focus on learning new ones.

☐ **Playing Different Dynamic Levels**
  - *Forte*
  - *Mezzo Piano*

☐ **Connected Tones – *Legato***

☐ **Detached Tones – *Staccato***

☐ **Playing in Extended Position**

NEW!

Balance between Melody and Accompaniment
Play the *legato* melody with more arm weight by leaning into the keys. Play the *staccato* accompaniment with less arm weight, releasing the keys as soon as you play them.

Warm-Ups

Clown Capers *pg. 16*

Have you ever watched circus clowns frolic around the arena? Some leap in large arcs from foot to foot while others jump lightly up and down.

Play the left hand *legato* and ***mf*** passing the sound from finger to finger. Play the right hand *staccato* and ***p*** releasing the keys as soon as you play them.

Shifting Gears *pg. 17*

Many sports ask you to change quickly from one kind of movement to another. For example, in basketball you dribble the ball as fast as possible down the court, then stop quickly to shoot a basket. This kind of quick change in movement is often called "shifting gears." To do this well, you need to plan ahead.

Prepare to "shift gears" between the slurs and *staccatos* by mastering the different motions in each hand.

Clown Capers

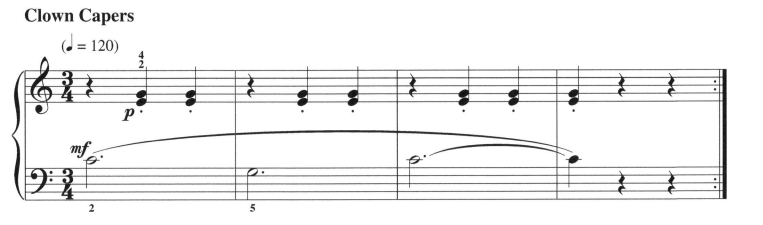

Shifting Gears

Clown Capers

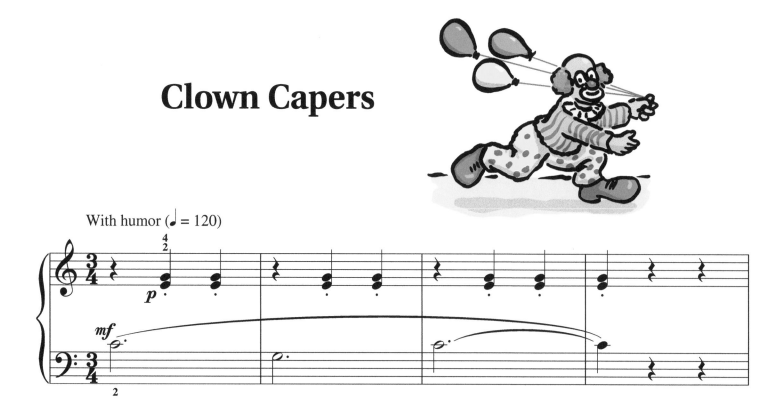

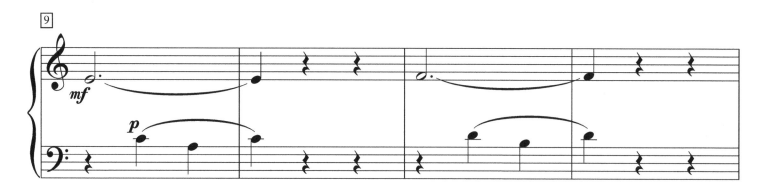

Shifting Gears

Allegro

Accompaniment (Student plays one octave higher than written.)

Allegro (♩ = 150)

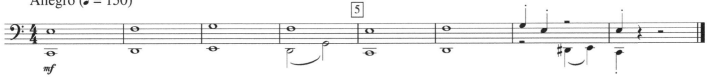

17

Musical Fitness Plan

Use this checklist to review fitness skills and to focus on learning new ones.

☐ **Playing Different Dynamic Levels**
- *Forte*
- *Mezzo Forte*
- *Mezzo Piano*
- *Piano*

☐ **Playing *Crescendo* and *Decrescendo***

☐ **Connected Tones – *Legato***

☐ **Detached Tones – *Staccato***

NEW!

Playing Black and White Keys Together in the Same Hand

Press both keys into the keybed with equal arm weight so the tones sound at the same time. Move your hand slightly forward for comfort.

NEW!

Using the Damper Pedal

Press the damper pedal down with your right foot, keeping your heel on the floor.

Warm-Ups

Habañera *pg. 20*

The opera "Carmen" (1875) by French composer Georges Bizet is set in Spain. Carmen, the leading character in the story, dances a Habañera. The ♩. ♪♩ rhythm pattern is often found in Spanish music.

Keep the ♩. ♪♩ rhythm steady by dropping your arm weight into the first note of the three-note phrase. Shift the weight from 1-5 or 5-1 by rotating your wrist. Release the quarter note as soon as you play it.

The Aquarium *pg. 21*

Imagine two fish gliding through their watery home, imitating each others' motions as they swim.

Play the melodic intervals in each hand with a drop/lift motion of the wrist.

Play the harmonic intervals so that both tones sound at exactly the same time. Press both keys into the key bed with equal arm weight.

Use the damper pedal throughout to blend the sounds.

Habañera

The Aquarium

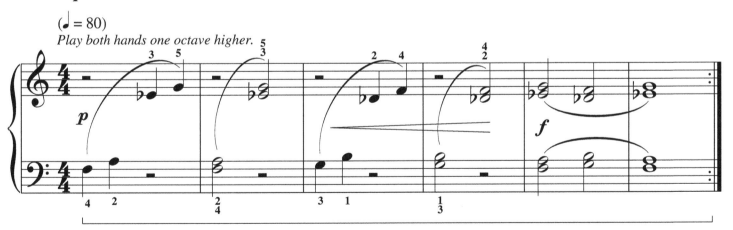

Habañera

Strictly

Accompaniment (Student plays both hands one octave lower than written.)

Strictly (♩ = 126)

The Aquarium

Expressively (♩ = 90)

Play both hands one octave higher.

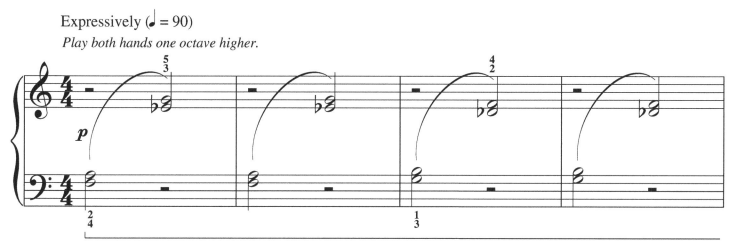

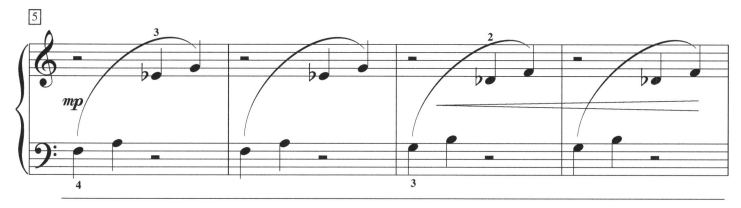

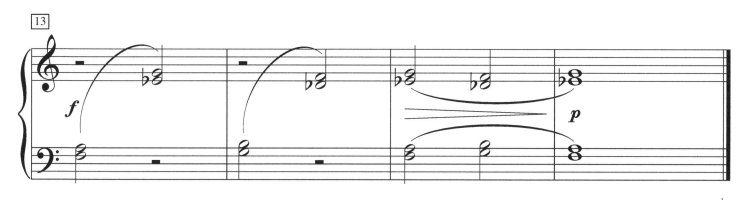

Use with Lesson Book 3, pg. 23

Musical Fitness Plan

Use this checklist to review fitness skills and to focus on learning new ones.

☐ **Playing Different Dynamic Levels**
- *Forte*
- *Mezzo Forte*
- *Mezzo Piano*
- *Piano*

☐ **Playing *Crescendo* and *Decrescendo***

☐ **Connected Tones – *Legato***

☐ **Detached Tones – *Staccato***

☐ **Using the Damper Pedal**

NEW!

Playing Chords
Listen for each chord tone to sound at exactly the same moment. Drop into each chord with full arm weight, balancing it equally over each finger.

NEW!

Playing Hand over Hand Arpeggios
As soon as you finish playing the left-hand broken chord, begin crossing your left hand over your right hand.

To the Teacher: *Demonstrate these warm-ups first. This will allow students to focus on the purely physical aspects of learning a new skill.*

Warm-Ups

Over And Over *pg. 24*

When learning a new skill, it helps to practice it over and over. It is important to keep your mind, body, eye, and ear connected as you play each repetition.

Play each blocked chord *staccato* with a lightly bouncing wrist. Listen carefully. Each chord tone must sound at exactly the same time.

A Long Way *pg. 25*

When we want to get a hold of something a long way away, we plant our feet firmly on the ground, use our eyes to judge the distance between us and the object, and then reach for it.

Before you begin, place your RH third finger on treble C so it will be ready to play in measure 3. Position your LH over the low bass A and E. Use your eyes to judge the distance from low A to the A below middle C. Using your fifth finger as a guide, practice reaching from low A to the A below middle C. Now you are ready to play **A Long Way**.

Over And Over

($\quad$ = 140)

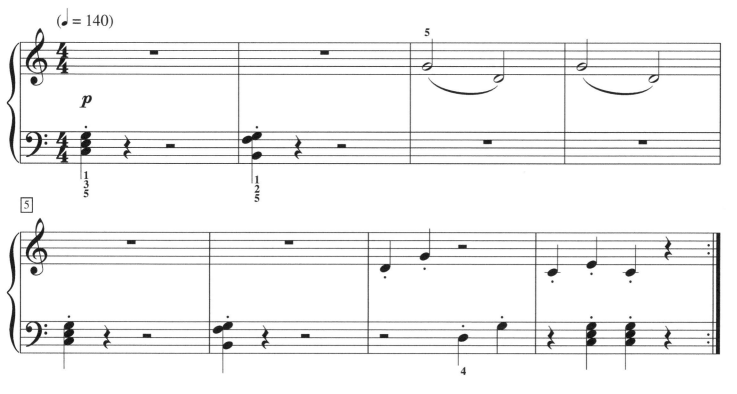

A Long Way

($\quad$ = 63)

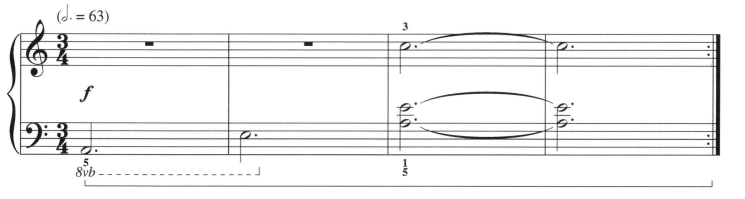

Over And Over

Steady (♩ = 150)

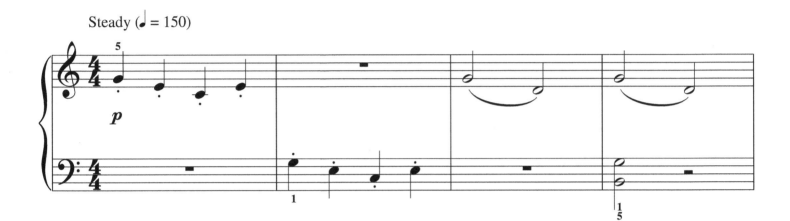

A Long Way

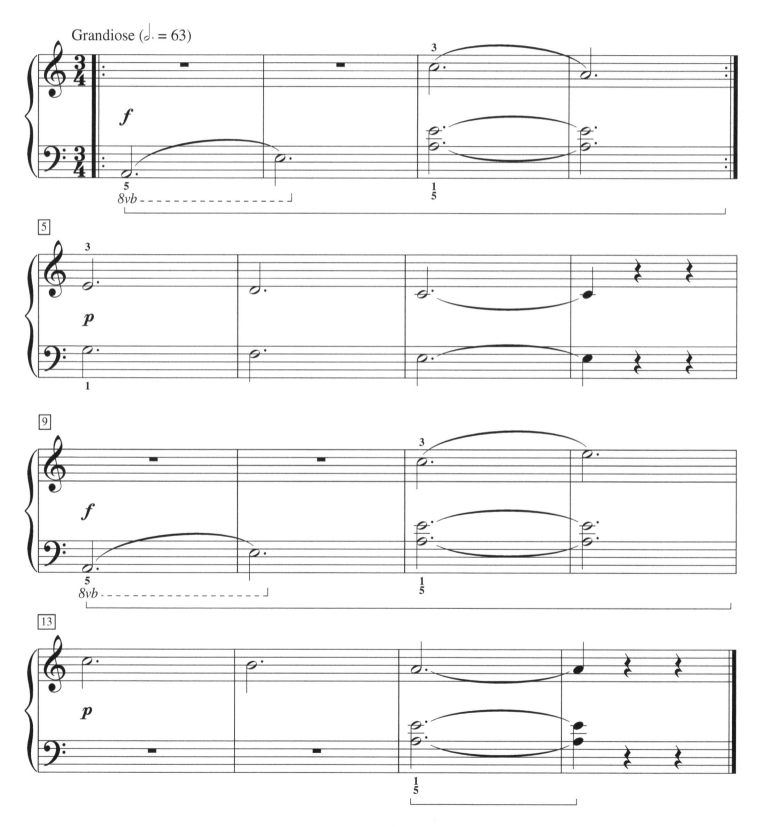

Use with Lesson Book 3, pgs. 32-33

Musical Fitness Plan

Use this checklist to review fitness skills and to focus on learning new ones.

- ☐ **Playing Different Dynamic Levels**
  - *Forte*
  - *Mezzo Forte*
  - *Mezzo Piano*
  - *Piano*

- ☐ **Connected Tones – *Legato***

- ☐ **Detached Tones – *Staccato***

- ☐ **Playing Black and White Keys Together in the Same Hand**

- ☐ **Playing Chords**

- ☐ **Playing in Extended Position**

Warm-Ups

Slumber Bed *pg. 28*

When parents sing their baby to sleep at night, they might sing together in harmony. The mother sings one pitch while the father sings a different pitch at the same time. Each has to listen carefully to his part so he doesn't begin singing the other's pitch by mistake.

When two hands play different notes at the same time, concentrate on the finger numbers and on the direction in which each hand moves—up together, down together, or in contrary motion. It helps to practice the music away from the piano, first tapping the notes with your fingers on the keyboard cover.

Jam *pg. 29*

In jazz, "jam" has another meaning: "to improvise with several other players."

Use your fifth finger to pass the sound as smoothly as possible between the half steps. Let your hand shift in and out slightly as you play this white-key/black-key pattern.

Keep your thumb close to the keys on the repeated notes.

Slumber Bed

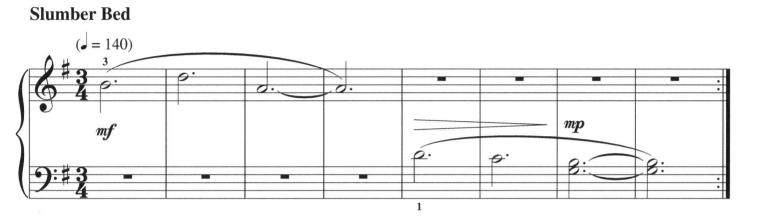

Jam

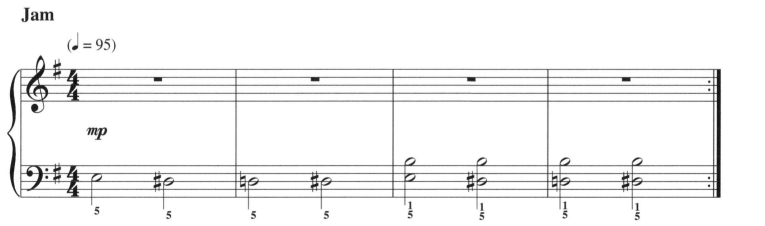

Slumber Bed

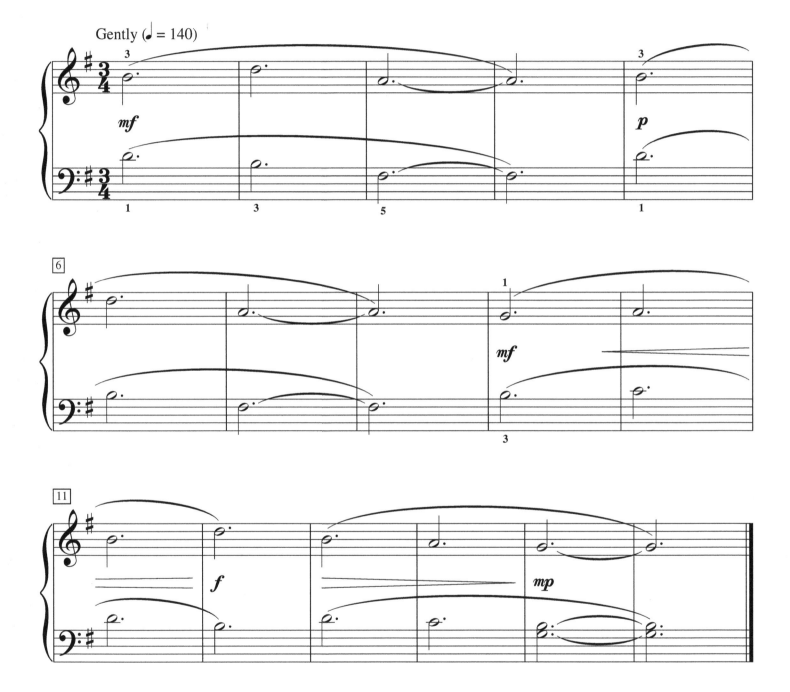

Jam

Slow and jazzy, with a swing ($\quarternote$ = 105)

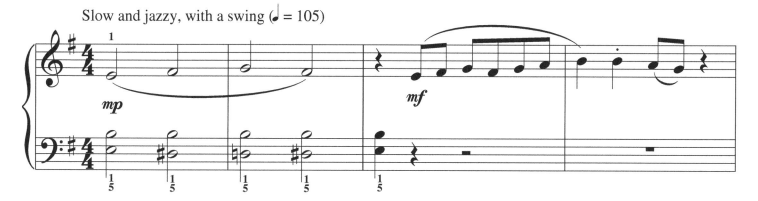

Musical Fitness Plan

Use this checklist to review fitness skills and to focus on learning new ones.

- ☐ **Playing Different Dynamic Levels**
  - *Mezzo Forte*
  - *Mezzo Piano*
  - *Piano*

- ☐ **Connected Tones –** *Legato*

- ☐ **Detached Tones –** *Staccato*

- ☐ **Playing in Extended Position**

- ☐ **Playing Black and White Keys Together in the Same Hand**

- ☐ **Playing Chords**

To the Teacher: Demonstrate these warm-ups first. This will allow students to focus on the purely physical aspects of learning a new skill.

Warm-Ups

Quiet Moments *pg. 32*

Quiet moments give us a chance to daydream. When we feel dreamy, we move slowly and softly.

Create a peaceful mood by using less arm weight to make a *mezzo-piano* sound and by playing in a slow tempo.

Practice in two-measure phrases, shaping the notes into a musical conversation between the hands. Play each phrase with a drop/lift motion of the arm and wrist.

Careful Steps *pg. 33*

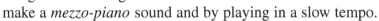

When tiptoeing on uneven surfaces, we keep our legs the same length by bending our knees and moving from surface to surface with as little body movement as possible.

When playing a black key and a white together in the same hand, keep your fingers rounded and close to the fallboard so you can move easily from one combination of keys to the other.

Quiet Moments

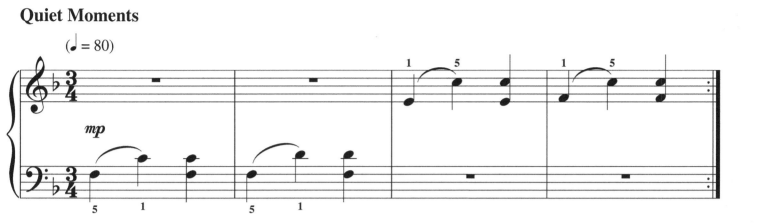

Careful Steps

Quiet Moments

Smoothly (♩ = 100)

mp

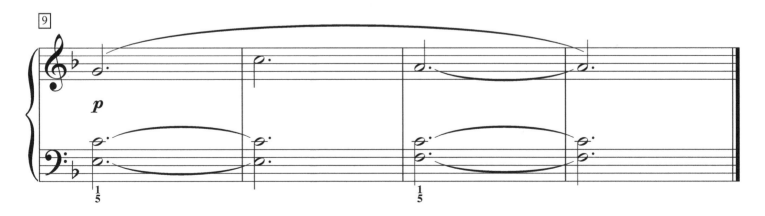

p

Careful Steps

Steady (♩ = 92)

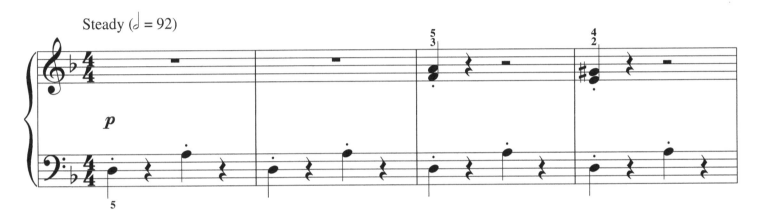

33

Use with Lesson Book 3, pgs. 46-47

Musical Fitness Plan

Use this checklist to review fitness skills and to focus on learning new ones.

☐ **Playing Different Dynamic Levels**
- *Forte*
- *Mezzo Forte*
- *Mezzo Piano*

☐ **Playing *Decrescendo***

☐ **Accents**

☐ **Playing Chords**

☐ **Playing in Extended Position**

NEW!

Changing Positions
When moving from one position to another, use your thumb or fifth finger as a guide. Look ahead. Plan your move to the new position.

Warm-Ups

Spike's Blues *pg. 36*

The Blues is a type of American popular music that began in the first decade of the 20th century. An important feature of the blues style is a 12-bar harmonic pattern.

C / C / C / C　　F / F / C / C　　G / F / C / C

In **Spike's Blues**, you will play the accompaniment. Jazz musicians call this "comping." You will "comp" while your teacher plays the melody using a C "blues scale."

During the rests, move your hands to each new position (C, F, or G) quickly and easily.

Sleep-Over *pg. 37*

Everyone likes to spend some time "jamming" on the piano at a sleep-over. Has one of your friends ever taught you a version of this piece?

Let your right-hand thumb guide you to each new chord position.

Spike's Blues

($\quad$ = 100)

Play right hand one octave lower.

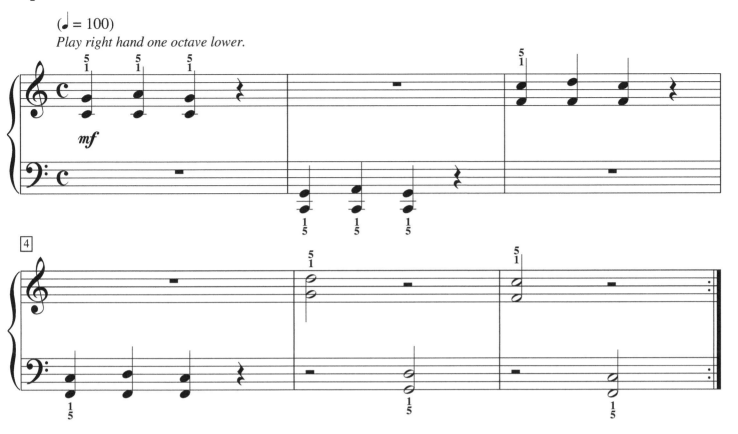

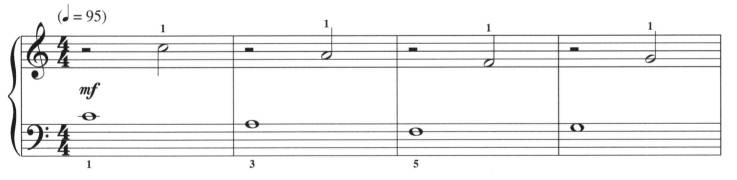

Sleep-Over

($\quad$ = 95)

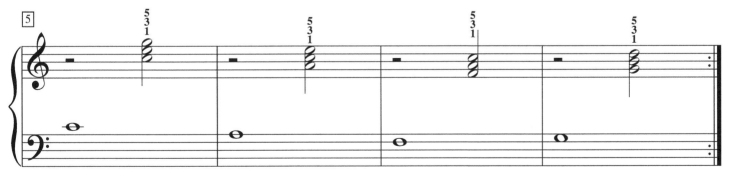

Spike's Blues

Slow Blues
Play right hand one octave lower throughout.

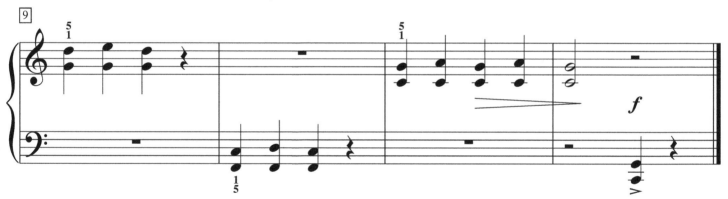

Accompaniment

Slow Blues ($\quarternote$ = 110) ($\eighthnote\eighthnote$ = $\quarternote\eighthnote$)

Sleep-Over

With soul, swing eighths
Play both hands one octave lower throughout.

Accompaniment
With soul, swing eighths (♩ = 105) (♫ = ♩³♪)

Use with Lesson Book 3, pg. 51

Musical Fitness Plan

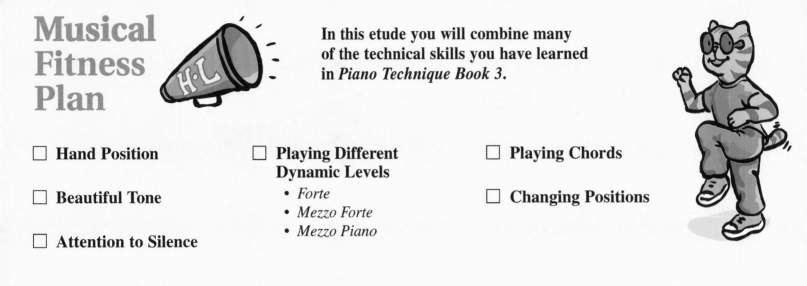

In this etude you will combine many of the technical skills you have learned in *Piano Technique Book 3*.

☐ **Hand Position**

☐ **Beautiful Tone**

☐ **Attention to Silence**

☐ **Playing Different Dynamic Levels**
  • *Forte*
  • *Mezzo Forte*
  • *Mezzo Piano*

☐ **Playing Chords**

☐ **Changing Positions**

Warm-Up

Cut And Paste *pg. 37*

When you compose a paragraph on your computer, you can cut and paste it from one location to another.

In **Cut And Paste**, the musical patterns repeat each time in a new position. The warm-up will help you learn to move from one position to another on time and with ease.

Cut And Paste

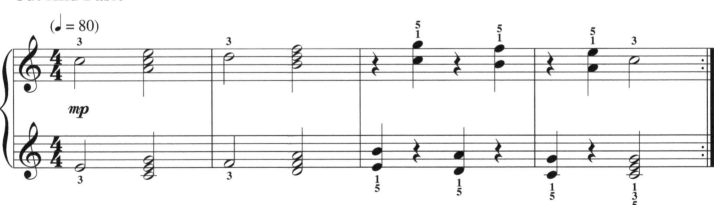

Cut And Paste

Andante (♩ = 90)

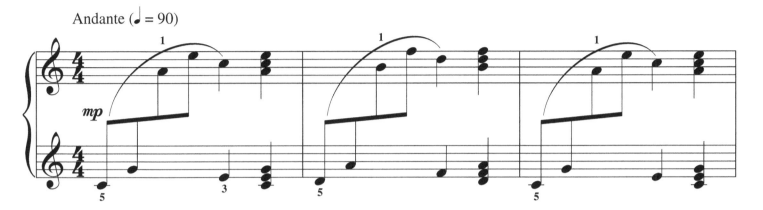

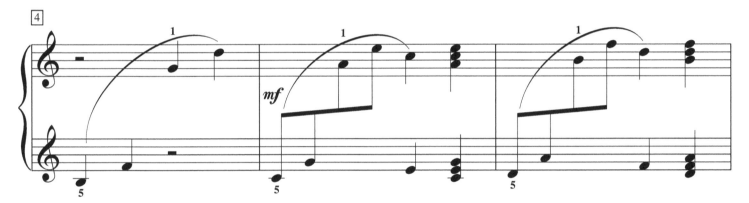

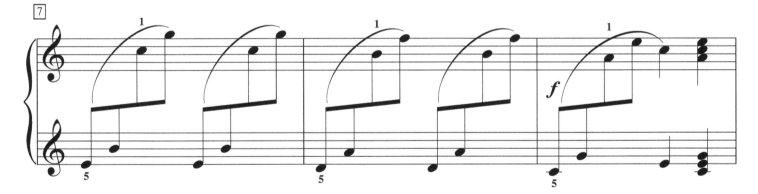

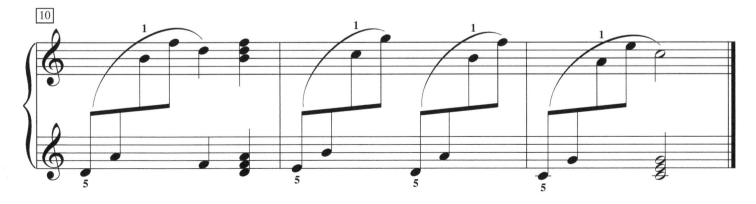

Use with Lesson Book 3, pgs. 54-55

Five-Finger Patterns

Play these exercises hands separately and then hands together in the following keys:

C Major / C Minor	**G Major / G Minor**	**F Major / F Minor**
A Minor / A Major	**E Minor / E Major**	**D Minor / D Major**

Play each one using these dynamics: *p - mp - mf - f*

Play each one at the following tempi: ♩ = 70; ♩ = 80; ♩ = 90; ♩ = 120.

Play the blue, unstemmed notes in one quick impulse before each beat, using a drop/lift motion of the wrist.